AF504396

Pinky The Lost Peacock In A Unique World

pinkythepeacock.com

Copyright © 2024

By Juan J. Williams

Follow us on Social Media

Scan To Follow us on Social Media

https://www.instagram.com/officialpinkythepeacock

Youtube: https://youtube.com/@pinkythepeacock

TikTok: https://www.tiktok.com/@officialpinkythepeacock

Pinky was a young peacock
who had pink and blue feathers
that shone in the sunlight.
Pinky loved playing in her nest,
surrounded by leaves
and the whispers of the wind.

One sunny day, as Pinky twirled and danced
in her nest, a strong wind blew her far away from home

"Uh-oh! I'm flying!" Pinky screamed, flying without
control into the unknown.

Flapping her wings in confusion,
Pinky found herself in a place
unlike anything she had ever seen before.
Trees of all shapes and sizes surrounded her,
and the chirps,
hoots, and calls of strange creatures filled the air.
"Where am I?" Pinky whispered,
her heart fluttering with worry,
but there was no immediate answer.

"Mama?"
She called and cried
hoping to see her mom
but she was all alone.
She decided to keep walking
until she found her way home.
MAMAA...

Suddenly, she saw a slow-moving tortoise.
She became confused and frightened.

Pinky, with wide eyes, stammered,
"Oh-oh my feathers!
Who are you, and
why are you so slow?"

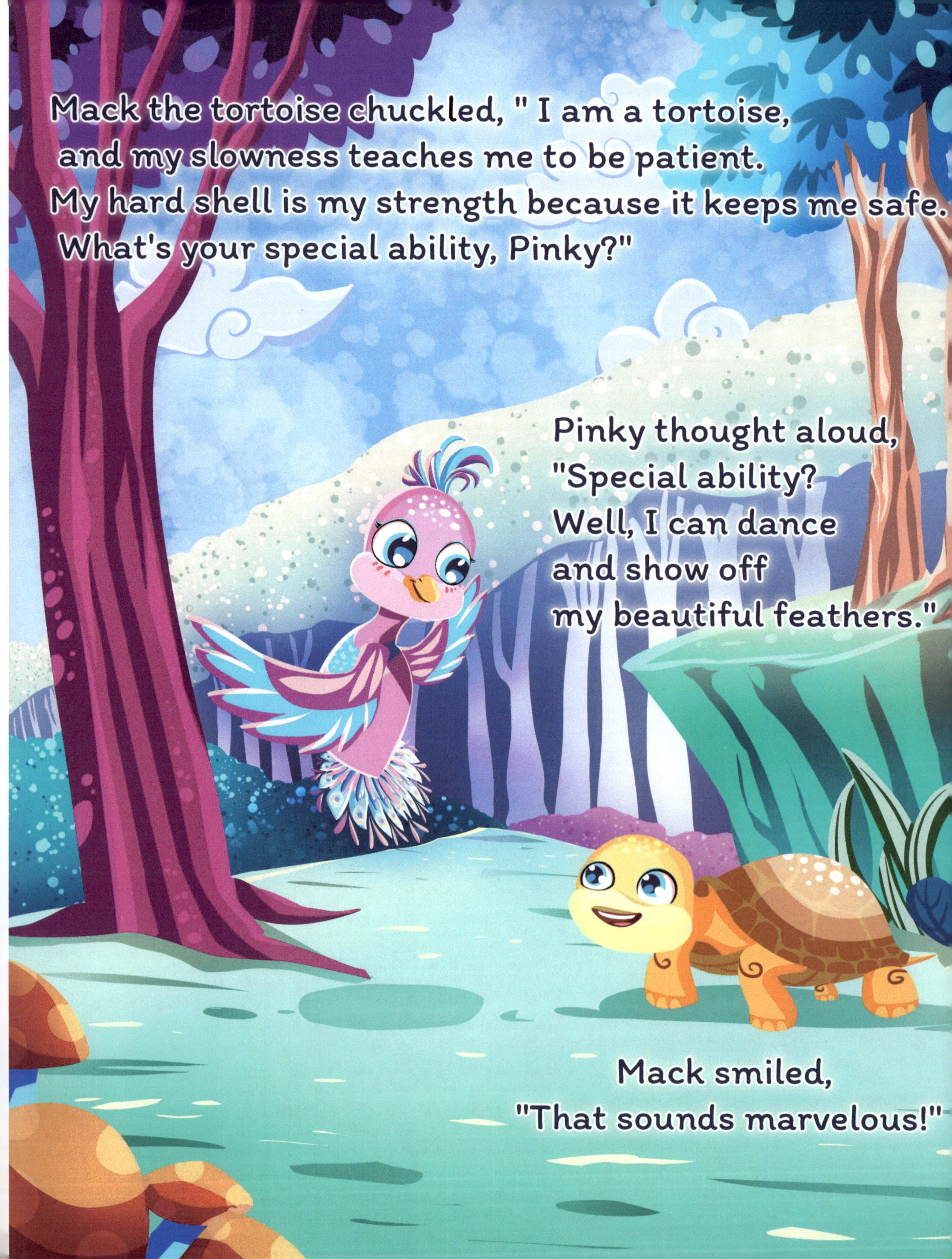

Mack the tortoise chuckled, " I am a tortoise, and my slowness teaches me to be patient. My hard shell is my strength because it keeps me safe. What's your special ability, Pinky?"

Pinky thought aloud, "Special ability? Well, I can dance and show off my beautiful feathers."

Mack smiled, "That sounds marvelous!"

Pinky paused before asking,
"But why am I so different from you?
Am I strange?"

Mack chuckled,
"Oh, my dear, differences make
the world more beautiful.
Your colorful feathers are your special gift,
just like my shell is mine."

Pinky's eyes widened and she became more curious.
She hoped to see other animals and find out how
different they were from her.

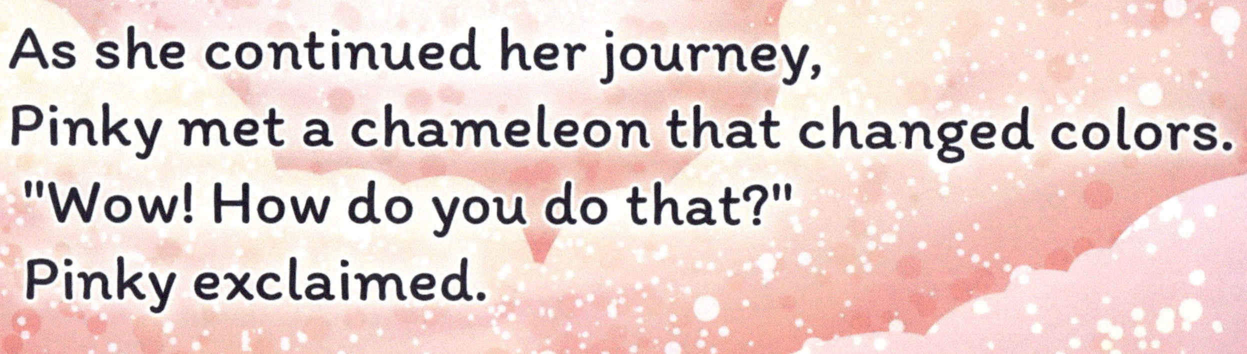

As she continued her journey,
Pinky met a chameleon that changed colors.
"Wow! How do you do that?"
Pinky exclaimed.

Camo the chameleon grinned,
"My color-changing
helps me blend in.
What about you, Pinky?"

Pinky thought and answered,
"I can't change colors,
but my feathers sparkle.
Maybe that's my special thing!"

As Pinky swung through the trees,
she saw a lively monkey.

"Hey there! Watch this!"
Loco the monkey
jumped from tree to tree easily.

Pinky, amazed, asked,
"Can you teach me to do that?"

Loco laughed,
"Sure thing, Pinky!
But first, tell me what makes you special."
Pinky giggled as she mimicked a few jumps,
imagining herself swinging through the forest,
"I'm special because I can twirl and dance."

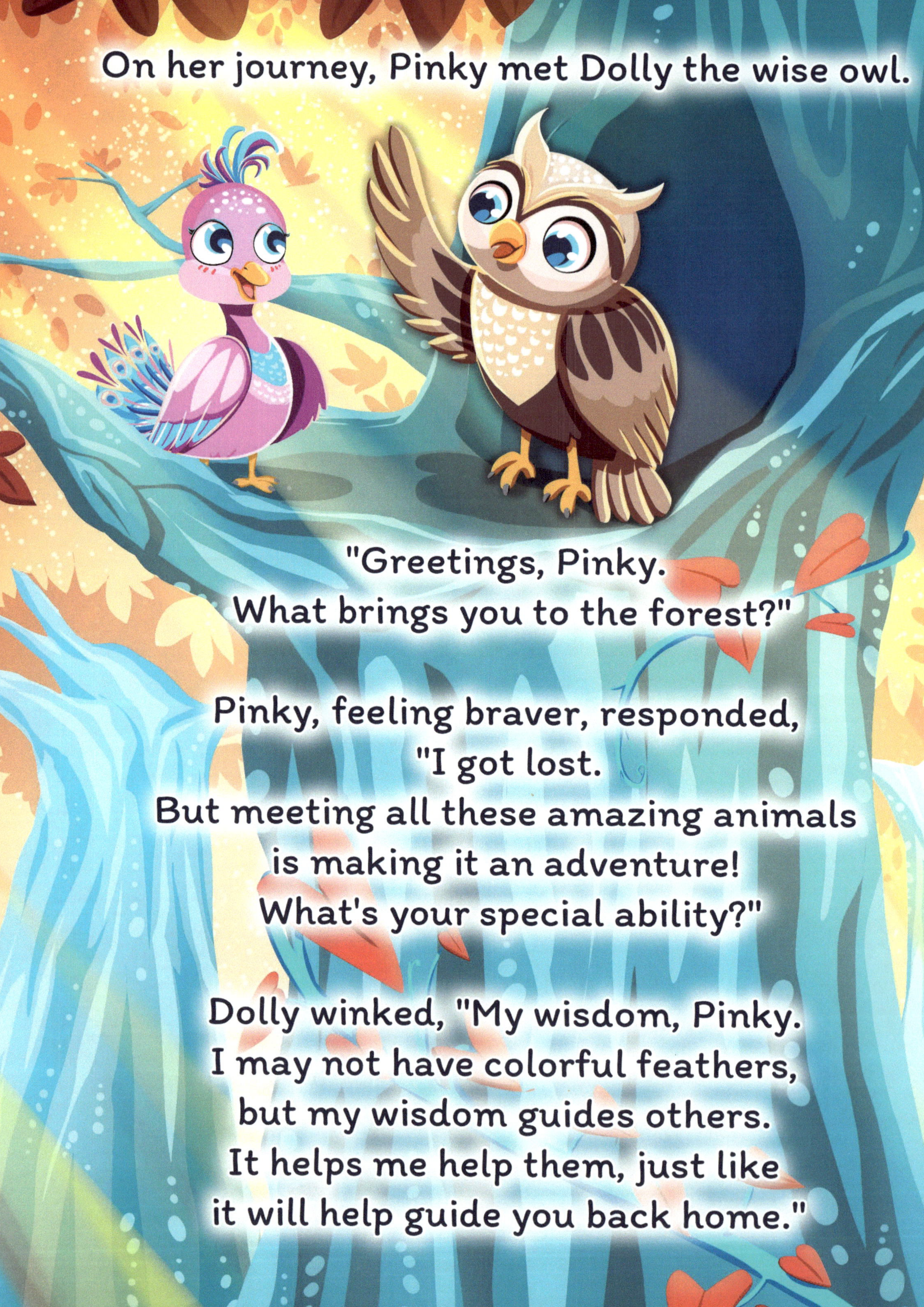

On her journey, Pinky met Dolly the wise owl.

"Greetings, Pinky.
What brings you to the forest?"

Pinky, feeling braver, responded,
"I got lost.
But meeting all these amazing animals
is making it an adventure!
What's your special ability?"

Dolly winked, "My wisdom, Pinky.
I may not have colorful feathers,
but my wisdom guides others.
It helps me help them, just like
it will help guide you back home."

As Pinky went deeper into the forest,
she began to feel a sense of belonging.

"Maybe I'm not odd;
maybe I'm just different,
like everyone else,"
Pinky said proudly.

Soon, Pinky made friends with smaller birds,
each with their unique melodies

And a long-necked giraffe.
"Your neck is so long!
Is it your special thing?"

Grant the giraffe smiled,
"Yes, I can reach the leaves at the top of the trees.
I'm sure you have your own special gifts too, Pinky!"

Pinky couldn't contain her excitement.
She continued to think about
the beauty of being different.

"This is so amazing!
I never knew there were
so many amazing creatures
in the forest.
Our differences really make us special
and help us contribute to the world."

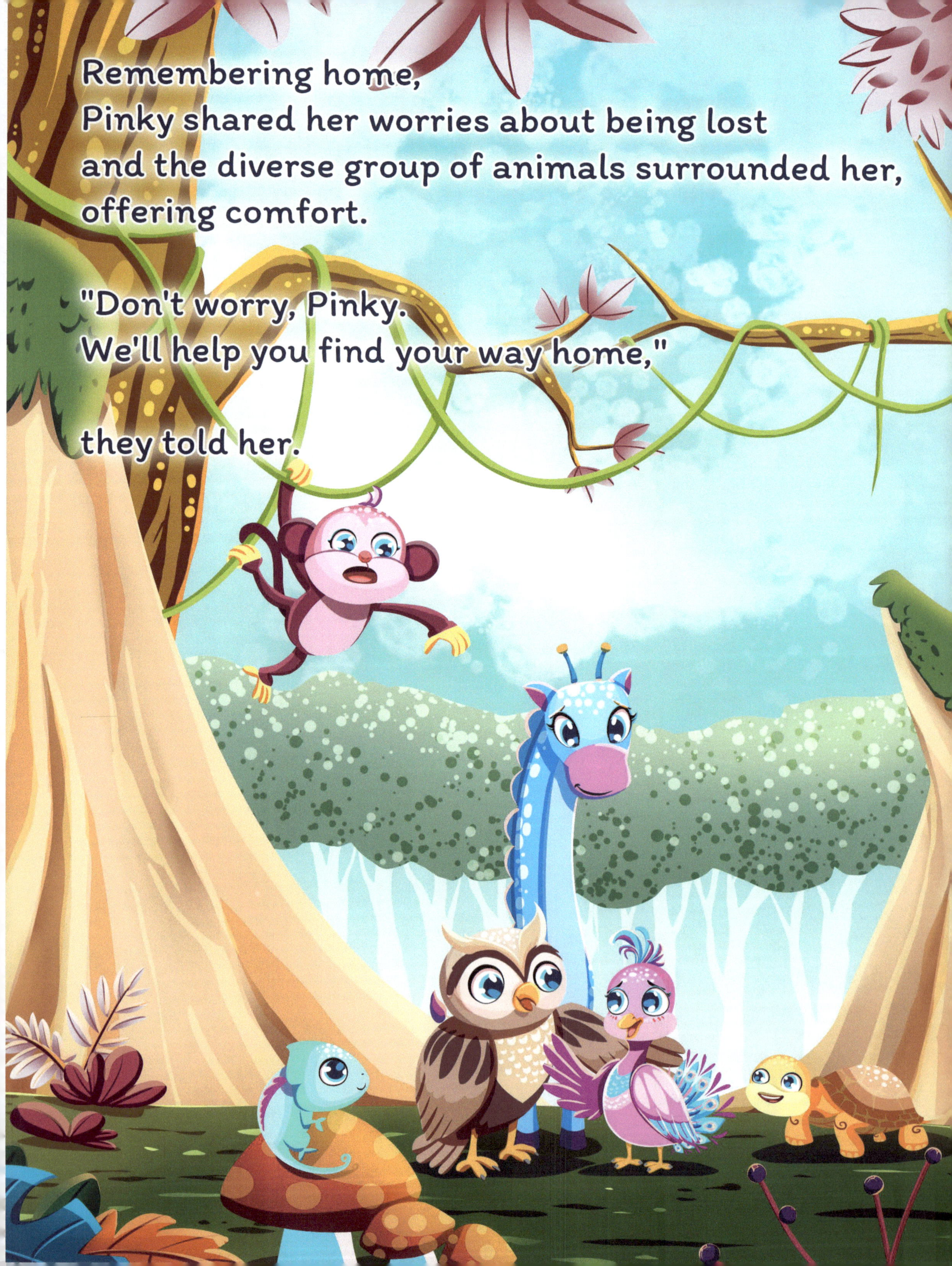

Remembering home,
Pinky shared her worries about being lost
and the diverse group of animals surrounded her,
offering comfort.

"Don't worry, Pinky.
We'll help you find your way home,"

they told her.

Together, the group of animals
shared clues and tools
that matched
their unique abilities.

Camo changed colors
to create a green path,
Loco swung through the trees
to look ahead for Pinky's home,
and Dolly provided guidance
on how to find her way.

With the help of her new friends,
Pinky joyously found herself back
at the branches of her nest.

"Oh my baby!
I'm so happy you found your way
back home!"
her mom shouted as she ran to hug Pinky.

She hugged her mother tightly,
tears of happiness rolling down her face.

"Thank you, Mom!
I met many animals and learned that even
though we're different, our unique gifts
make us special and amazing."

"Yes, everyone is not the same and that is
what makes our world interesting
and colorful,"

Pinky's mother smiled, realizing that
her daughter had not only found her way home
but had also discovered the importance
of accepting the differences of others.

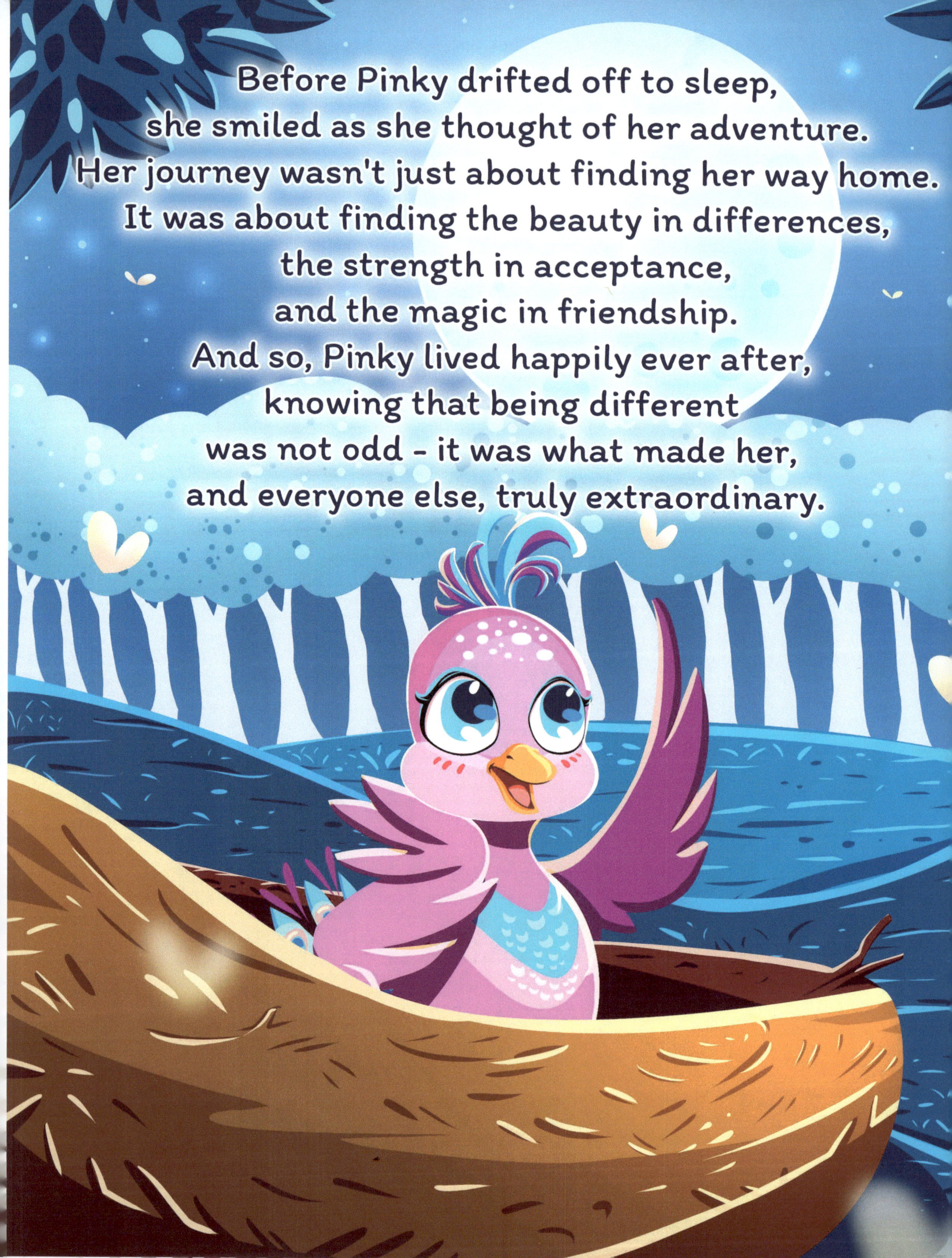
Before Pinky drifted off to sleep,
she smiled as she thought of her adventure.
Her journey wasn't just about finding her way home.
It was about finding the beauty in differences,
the strength in acceptance,
and the magic in friendship.
And so, Pinky lived happily ever after,
knowing that being different
was not odd - it was what made her,
and everyone else, truly extraordinary.

Glossary: Your Vocabulary Guide

1. **Ability**: The skill or talent to do something well. It's like being good at dancing, singing, or playing sports.

2. **Acceptance**: The act of welcoming and embracing someone or something as they are. It's when you are okay with people being different from you and treat them with kindness and respect.

3. **Adventure**: An exciting journey or experience. It's like going on a journey, quest or exploring something new and interesting.

4. **Belonging**: The feeling of being connected or fitting in. It's when you feel like you are a part of a group or place.

5. **Braver**: Feeling more courageous. It means you're not as scared as before, and you're ready to face something challenging.

6. **Clues**: Hints or pieces of information that help you figure something out, like solving a puzzle or mystery.

7. **Confusion**: Feeling lost or unsure. It's like when you don't know where you are or what to do.

8. **Contributions**: Things that someone gives or does to help It's like when you share or do something that makes things better.

9. **Curious**: Wanting to know more. It's that feeling you get see something interesting and you really want to find out about it.

10. **Diverse**: Different or varied. This word is used when there are many different things or people in one place.

11. **Extraordinary**: Very special or remarkable. It's used to describe something or someone that is amazing or unique.

12. **Frightened**: Feeling scared or afraid. It's the emotion you might have when something unexpected or scary happens.

13. **Guidance**: Help and advice that shows you the way or helps you make decisions. It's like having someone wise guide you.

14. **Imagining**: Creating pictures or ideas in your mind. It's when you think about things that aren't there or haven't happened yet, like imagining yourself as a superhero.

15. **Interesting**: Something that catches your attention or keeps you curious. It's when things are exciting or make you want to learn more.

16. **Mimicked**: Copying someone or something, by doing the same actions or saying the same words.

17. **Sparkle**: Shining brightly with small, flickering lights. It's like the glimmer or twinkle you might see in something beautiful.

18. **Stammer**: Speaking with interruptions or repeating sounds because of nervousness or uncertainty.

19. **Strange**: Unusual or different from what you're used to. It's when something is a bit odd or unfamiliar.

20. **Unique**: Being one of a kind, special, and different from anything else. Each person and thing has its own unique qualities.

Activity Section

After reading, "Pinky The Lost Peacock in a Unique World"

let's dive into some exciting activities to explore and celebrate our own uniqueness:

A. Questions From the Story:

1. Who is the main character in the story?

2. What problem does Pinky face at the beginning of the story?

3. Why does Pinky feel curious about the other animals she meets?

4. What are Pinky's special qualities?

5. How does Pinky's attitude change throughout the story?

B. Create Your Unique World

1. Let Out Your Imagination:

- Grab some paper, coloring pencils, markers, and let your imagination run wild.

- Design your own unique world filled with extraordinary creatures, just like Pinky's forest friends. What special abilities or features do they have?

2. Discover Your Unique Quality:

- Think about what makes you special and unique.

- Draw or write about your unique quality and how it can make the world more interesting.

3. Write Your Own Story:

●Use your creativity to write a short story about an adventure where your unique quality helps you overcome a challenge.

●Share your story with friends or family.

4. A Dance Party:

●Put on your favorite music and have a dance party! Show off your dance moves just like Pinky. Each dance move represents a unique quality you love about yourself.

5. Friendship Tree:

● Create a Friendship Tree by drawing a tree on paper.

- Write or draw the names of friends and family members who make your world colorful and special.

6. Share Your Adventure:

- Share your drawings, stories, or dance moves with others. You can create a mini-presentation or a showcase to celebrate everyone's uniqueness.

C.Guiding Questions:

- What did you discover about yourself during this activity?

- How did your unique quality shine in your created world or story?

"Remember, everyone is special in their own way,
and embracing our uniqueness makes the world
a brighter place.
Have fun exploring and celebrating
what makes you, YOU!"